THE
CUSTOMER CONUNDRUM

9 CRUCIAL STEPS
FOR WINNING CUSTOMERS
AND
OUTSMARTING YOUR COMPETITION

Gary L. Smith

Forward by Colleen Ferrary, Founder of Small Business USA

A catalogue record of this book is available from The Library of Congress.
ISBN: 978-0-9767619-0-7

Dedication

To three amazing women:
Alexandra, Ashleigh, and Jacqueline
They love the Lord and serve their patients and clients
with the highest levels of caring and service –

And to their mother,
Martha Shalling Smith
Who raised them with hearts prepared for service to others

Other Books by Gary Smith

The Shepherd & The Princess:
7 Keys To Conquering The Goliaths In Your Life
ISBN 978-1-291-43650-1

Achieving Unusual Greatness:
Timeless Lessons From The Trail Already Blazed
ISBN 978-1-304-57716-0

Gary also offers both a CD and mp3 download of an audio version of *The Shepherd and The Princess*

All books and audio products are available at www.optechs.com and include free shipping!

Praise For Gary's Books

Gary Smith has created an extremely interesting and personally rewarding "life coaching" book based on his insights from a very powerful biblical story, interspersed with his own life experiences. I found the book to be professionally stimulating as well as thought provoking. Gary is obviously a seasoned manager who blends together proven professional goal setting techniques with elements of his strong faith in a unique and very enjoyable and positive read.

Ron Cerny, President/CEO
Connor Sport Court International

I found this book both very informative and entertaining. The author uses a well-known bible tale to demonstrate a clear and concise approach to setting and achieving important life goals beyond what most of us usually achieve. This book is very well written with many personal insights into the author's own experiences that bring to life the books key principles. He also reveals many details of this Bible story not generally known, and makes it relevant to today. His writing style makes this an easy read and the author's affable personality is evident. I recommend this book highly to anyone seeking to significantly improve his or her life through goal setting and, more importantly, goal achievement.

Robert Linden, Operations Mgr. (retired)
Bicron Electronics Company

Gary has done another incredible job! From the moment you open the book, you know that this one is different. Gary's personal experiences, caring spirit, and study guide all work together to empower you with everything you need to reach your dreams and to become successful in those dreams. This book is easy to read and understand. With its study guide, it is also a book to reflect back on over and over. You won't read it and just put it down, forgetting most of it a day or two later. It's a book that will remain in your heart as you make it a part of your life and thinking process. Thank you, Gary, for this life-changing book.

Donna Mason, Founder
Summer Enterprises

This book contains solid foundational wisdom and truths that a person needs to begin his or her journey to a successful and meaningful life that will bring meaning and purpose. It is packed with the necessary homework and steps that, if performed and followed, will bring much success. Great book!

Phil Martinez, Chaplain
Milwaukee, WI

Meet Gary Smith

Gary Smith is a business and personal coach, business consultant, professional speaker, and author. He is the founder and president of Optimum Performance Technologies, LLC.

Gary shares his expertise and professionalism with his clients as he employs his years of experience as a problem solver and visionary leader. People are inspired and motivated by Gary's insights in the areas of human behavior and business dynamics. He has a keen ability to simplify, communicate, and apply effective strategies for creating positive, profitable, lasting results. Gary combines the elements of entertainment, education, and empowerment to lead the way to optimized performance.

An accomplished business professional with years of technical and executive experience, Gary has worked with some of the world's most prestigious and innovative companies. His expertise lies in a unique ability to increase productivity, performance, and profitability at all organizational levels.

Gary is an experienced business and personal coach and mentor who is deeply committed to the success of his clients. His caring demeanor and open sharing of his life experiences create an atmosphere of trust that facilitates the learning and achievement process. As a best-selling author and professional speaker, he shares a deep knowledge and understanding of business and personal development with his audiences in an energetic, fun, and informative way.

Gary is also a radio personality. He currently hosts The Gary Smith Show, a weekly broadcast on business and personal development, that airs every Saturday morning on WSDK, 1550 AM in Hartford, CT. Gary's show can be heard around the world via the Internet at www.wsdk1550.com.

Table of Contents

Forward (Foreword)

by **Colleen Ferrary**
President of Small Business USA
and Small Business Advisors of America

This forward has been such an honor for me to write. *Yes forward, not foreword.* I believe that if you're reading this book today, you are ready to move your business *forward*, so this is the first page and the first step to making that happen. As Gary Smith says in his book, he and I met because of the written word – a "word" that called him to action and prompted him to reach out. *I know this book will call you to action.* Its powerful message is reinforced with storytelling and structure to support your initiatives.

I grew up in a very customer-centric environment. At the height of my career, I had almost 5,000 employees and was responsible for nearly $1 billion in sales. We measured customer impact every year and in 100 different ways. Each time, several pieces of information were undeniable:

1. Giving customers what they want, when they want it, was the number one differentiator in sales.
2. Being nice to the customer and delivering a memorable experience created repeat business (loyalty) and continuous growth.
3. Positive shifts in customer satisfaction clearly aligned with increased transaction sizes.

Gary's very first story about Jane and her hair salon experience could apply to any one of us. We all deliver what we think is the best service, but how often do we challenge our own assumptions? Throughout his book, Gary shares examples of good and bad experiences that undoubtedly make a difference in whether customers come back.

Part of moving up in a company is that you move around. However, the story doesn't change. Wherever I've been, customer service is a primary need of the consumer. Studies have shown that only 1 in 20 consumers will voice discontent, even when they've had a horrible experience. To put it in perspective, if you've had one person complain to you, statistically there are 19 who will share their bad experience with at least 8 others, even though they've said *nothing* to you. That equates to 152 potential clients who may never do business with you because of your poor customer service. The next time you receive a customer complaint, I challenge you to think about the 152 negative comments you need to overcome with potential clients.

While living outside Connecticut, I would regularly come home to visit. Every time I visited, I would drive by three sandwich shops to go to Jean and Russ's sandwich shop. I had to wait in line and pay a dollar more to get a sandwich that wasn't really any better than I could get at another store. Why did I go out of my way to go there? Because the first day I walked into Jean and Russ's deli they made me feel special. They made me feel that they cared. They made me feel like family. More importantly, every time I returned they continued to treat me like family.

Several years later, Jean and Russ sold their business for quite an extraordinary amount of money, especially since it was just a sandwich shop. Along with the business, they sold their recipes, and the new owners retained the same staff. The only thing that "*changed*" in the business was that Jean and Russ retired.

One year later, the deli closed. The new owners lost their entire investment. Why? People no longer felt like they were family. That's customer service and the impact it can have on your business. And it doesn't matter if you're selling sandwiches, screws, legal services, or shoes.

As the founder and owner of Small Business USA and Small Business Advisors of America, I've seen the impact of poor customer service over and over. *Don't underestimate the value of Gary's message.*

Gary is an extremely gifted writer who has found a way to very easily and simply create a roadmap for you to follow to change the course of customer service in your business. His message about "peeking behind the curtain" resonates with me, both today and from my past experiences. How many small businesses have poor customer service and don't realize it? The number is exceptionally high.

During my time with Target Stores, we would often look closely at stores with both underperforming customer service scores and sales. As we tried to ferret out the reasons for the poor results, we often "peeked behind the curtain" using surveillance equipment. After doing this for a while, one is no longer surprised by what one finds. What we did find, however, was that in every single situation there were appalling gaps in customer service. Most of the time, when we fixed the gaps, we fixed the issues with sales.

Gary Smith is a brilliant consultant and I'm honored to know him. He has solved many problems and does so with organized diligence while staying focused on setting up business owners for success. His words and his nine point strategy resonate for every company we support, and for every major corporation I have ever known.

I encourage you to read this book, share the stories with your team, and re-read it every year. It's time to take customer service personally, and Gary has given you the tools to do just that.

Here's to your success! Time to move *forward!*

Prologue

As consumers, we all have stories to tell about poor customer service.

- The rude teller at the bank who's slow and grumpy
- The website at your favorite store where it's impossible to find the one product for which you're desperately searching
- The computer technician in India who barely speaks English
- Waiting on hold for an eternity until you finally get through the telephone queue, only to encounter a customer service person who can't help you

Virtually every individual I've met has a bad customer service experience to share.

Here's the $64,000 question:

If, as consumers, we've had one or more bad customer service experiences, why, as business owners, do we not do something to insure that our customers never have any reason to tell negative stories about us and our organizations?

In answering this question, we must be mindful that, thanks to the Internet and social media, the impact of customer dissatisfaction can be felt far more rapidly and broadly as people share negative experiences with their friends and business and personal networks.

This book provides many of the critical answers you've been seeking. Contained in the pages of the printed or electronic document you now hold in your hands is a healthy dose of my "secret sauce" for creating an organizational culture that will:

- Delight customers and transform them into advocates – sales people – for your business
- Give you all the leverage you need to thoroughly outsmart and confound your competition

Read on and begin infusing your business with a "delight thy customer" attitude!

To your health and success!!

Gary Smith
Southington, CT
July 2014

PART ONE

SETTING THE STAGE

The Customer Conundrum & The Goal of this Book

CHAPTER ONE
The Customer Conundrum

As a consultant, business and personal coach, professional speaker, and author, I am a student of people and their behaviors in a variety of very interesting circumstances. And as someone who has been involved in many aspects of customer contact and management for many years, I have seen the best, and the worst, of customer service. All one has to do is to keep ones eyes and ears open every time one goes to the grocery store, stops at the bank, shops online, or calls customer support to try to resolve an issue. Instances of poor, inadequate – or as Clark Howard terms it – "customer no service" – are rampant.

Customer service happens on two primary levels. These levels are **business – to – consumer** and **business – to – business**. Let's take a look at some examples of each.

Business – To – Consumer

In this arena, poor customer service can range from the very simple to the more complex and troubling.

- How about when you go to the bank? Ever stopped by to make a quick deposit or cash a check, only to find that the teller woke up on the wrong side of the bed? Did he just ignore you or mess up the transaction, or did he make Oscar The Grouch look like Shirley Temple?

- How about when you stop at your local fast food restaurant to get your morning coffee? One interesting scenario is when a patron specifically orders an extra large hazelnut with cream only. Ten seconds later, the clerk asks if she'd like cream and sugar in her coffee. She repeats that she only wants cream – and – you guessed it – when she finally gets her coffee, it has both cream and sugar.

Admittedly, you may look at these two examples and say, under your breath, "What's the big deal? This stuff happens all the time!" My question is, "Why does it happen at all?"

Let's take a look at a more serious example:

- Your personal computer fails to operate one morning and you have a major presentation in four hours. You hastily call the technical support number for the major computer manufacturer where you purchased your laptop. After spending forty-five minutes on hold listening to a combination of elevator music and advertisements touting how wonderful this company's equipment is – while you sit there with a non-functioning unit – you are, at long last, greeted by a technical service representative. You instantly recognize that this person is in a foreign country, either by his accent or by the poor phone connection. In addition, you quickly learn that he either barely speaks English or, if he does speak English, his speech is so heavily accented that you can only grasp every fourth or fifth word. And, to top it all off, if you happen to be a bit of a techie, like me, it takes you less than a minute to realize that his level of technical competence is non-existent.

Business – To – Business

This arena is similar to B2C, but it can be more complex. Consider the following:

Company "A" manufactures a widget that it sells to company "B". Company "B" is not happy with the quality of the product and has, for the past six months, been regularly rejecting batches of product to company "A" for either rework or replacement.

Company "A" hires me to help solve the problem. In my initial interview with company "A's" president, he explains that his company has a pristine quality record and that all of the quality documents they have indicate that the product shipped to company "B" fully met the specifications. He firmly believes that the issue is being caused by company "B", and that either their specifications are incorrect, it as a problem being caused by another component in the assembly (manufactured by someone else, of course), or that company "B" is damaging company "A's" product in the assembly process. Company "A's" president wants me to have a meeting with company "B" and "set them straight".

Before I agree to a meeting with company "B", I ask for the opportunity to familiarize myself with the manufacturing process being used by company "A" to produce the widget in question. After a quick review of the manufacturing process, I meet with the management team and suggest that we need to do a more detailed analysis of company "A's" manufacturing process. When they challenge me and say that doing so is a waste of time, I give them a few facts:

- They are using a statistical sampling plan to verify final product quality.
- The effectiveness and accuracy of any statistical sampling plan is predicated upon:
  - A stable manufacturing process
  - That is running in control (i.e., within defined limits for things like speed, time, and temperature)
  - That has been validated within normal process variation windows (i.e., if the process temperature can vary by 10 degrees, they have verified that the process will produce product within specifications at the upper and lower temperature extremes).
- I further note that, in instances where product fails final inspection, company "A" utilizes 100% inspection to verify product quality prior to shipment. I explain that 100% inspection is, at the very best, 85% effective so, in my opinion, there is a high probability that company "A" is indeed shipping defective product to their customer.

The Attitude of Business Owners

Let's contrast the above scenarios with the attitudes of business owners and leaders around the country. As I travel and work with companies and individuals, I always ask them this question:

Do you agree that the customer is one of the most important components of your business?

I always get unanimous agreement. Hands are raised and heads nod in affirmation. In the past sixteen years, I have never once had a business owner or senior manager disagree with this statement.

So – that brings us to a pivotal question:

If every business owner realizes and affirms the importance of the customer to his business, then why do we have so many dissatisfied customers?

Therein lies the disconnect – **The Customer Conundrum.**

In my opinion, there are only four reasons for the gap that exists between what business owners say and the level of customer dissatisfaction that exists in the world today:

1. Owners and leaders give lip service to the importance of the customer, but are not actively doing anything to please the customer.

2. Owners and leaders are trying to provide a high level of customer service, but there is a disconnect between what they are doing and what their customers need.

3. Owners and leaders still see customer service as a department and not a business philosophy that must permeate their organizations.

4. Owners and leaders are trying to provide high levels of customer service, but don't know all of the focal areas on which they should be touching.

This book has been written to address all four of these issues and to help you get your organization on the fast track to delighting your customers. By the end of this book, you will be equipped with all of the tools you need to transform your customers into patrons who are so happy with the products and services you provide that you will:

*   Consistently win more business from your current clients
*   Enjoy a wealth of referral business from your existing customer base

In addition to creating winning (and profitable) customer relationships, you'll also be strategically and tactically positioned to outsmart your competition at every turn of the winding, and sometimes treacherous, business road.

Turn the page and read on. Your pathway to excellent customer service lies just ahead!

CHAPTER TWO
Your Customers

Let me ask you several foundational questions:

1. Do you have customers?
2. How many customers do you have?
3. Are your customers undyingly loyal to you and your business?
4. Are you sure?
5. How do you know?

Jane Handly, a woman who's been involved in the customer service industry for over 25 years, tells a story with a very pointed meaning. Allow me to recount this brief story to you as best as I can recall it.

Jane is a blond – by choice. As a result, she visits her hairdresser every couple of months to make sure that the color of her hair remains consistent (i.e. to eliminate the dark roots). Jane had been seeing the same hairdresser for many years. She was pleased with the results she got from this particular woman, and the $60 she was charged for each treatment seemed reasonable to her.

One day, Jane decided that she had an urgent need for a visit to her hairdresser. However, when she made a phone call to get an appointment, she discovered that the woman was on vacation and wouldn't be returning for several weeks. Jane didn't feel that she could wait that long, so she made an appointment at another salon.

When she arrived at the salon, the receptionist came out from behind her desk, shook hands with her, and welcomed her to the establishment. At that point, Jane was shocked and thought to herself, "I should have asked in advance how much this was going to cost me!" The receptionist then told her, "Please come with me and I'll introduce you to the chemical technician who will be coloring your hair today."

At this point, Jane became really concerned that she had entered a very high-end salon, and that it was going to cost her a small fortune. She quickly checked her pocketbook to see if she had her credit card.

Jane had her hair colored and was then introduced to another woman who washed and styled her hair. While this lady was finishing her work, another woman came over, introduced herself as the cosmetologist, and said, "Oh, dear! We messed up your make-up. Let me touch that up for you."

Finally, just as Jane was getting ready to go to the front of the salon and pay what she assumed was going to be an enormous bill, another woman approached her, introduced herself, said she was the manicurist, gave her a business card, and said that she'd love to do her nails sometime.
Now remember, Jane had been paying $60 to get her hair colored. Guess how much this new salon charged her. $100? $150? No! Her bill was $45!!

Now here's the main question: **Did Jane switch hairdressers?** Yes, she did. In fact, Jane said she would have switched if the price had been $75!

Here's another important question. **What did Jane's original hairdresser do wrong?** ABSOLUTELY NOTHING!! Jane was happy with the service she had been receiving, and with the price she had been charged – *until she had a new customer service experience*.

The point of this little story is obvious. Customers are fickle. You don't have to do anything wrong to lose a customer. All the customer has to do is have a different, and perhaps more attentive or pleasurable experience somewhere else – and they're gone! As business owners, this means that we must:

- Be creative in serving our customers. We must nurture the relationships, communicate with them, and never give them a reason to go anywhere else. As an example, if Jane's original hairdresser had called her a month in advance of her planned vacation, let Jane know that she was going to be away for a few weeks, and set an appointment to take care of Jane's hair before she left – would Jane have had any reason to look anywhere else? NO!

- Constantly see what our competition is doing and strive to outsmart them by doing more innovative things to please our customers.

Customers are indeed fickle. They are hard to get and hard to keep. But successful business owners know that it is far easier to keep an existing customer than it is to attract and cultivate a new one.

CHAPTER THREE
The Infusion Pump Approach

In much of the consulting and many of the talks that I give, I mention the word "*infusion*" in conjunction with customer service. Before I have the opportunity to explain what I mean, I begin to get some puzzled looks, so let me explain what I refer to as *The Infusion Pump Approach*.

If you look up the word "infusion" in the dictionary, you will find the following:

"The addition of something (such as money) that is needed or helpful."

Two of my three daughters work in the medical field, so I am familiar with the term infusion pump. I looked up the definition and found this:

"An infusion pump is a medical device that is used to deliver fluids into a patient's body in a controlled manner."

Combining these two definitions creates my definition of *The Infusion Pump Approach*, and that is:

The infusion pump approach is a method by which needed or helpful ideas and   methodologies are delivered, and allowed to permeate an organization, in a controlled manner, in order to effect permanent, positive change and create greater well being, growth, and profitability in that organization.

Let's take this statement apart and examine each element in light of *The Customer Conundrum*.

1. **The infusion pump approach is a "method".** The word method implies that there must be some kind of systematic approach to the infusion process. There must be a plan, a focus, and targeted action if success is to be achieved.

2. **By which needed or helpful ideas and methodologies are delivered**. The method in #1 provides the framework upon which we hang those things that the organization needs to employ to deliver better customer service. If you have ever been to an Asian restaurant and ordered a Pu Pu platter, you'll get this analogy. Because a Pu Pu platter contains a variety of appetizers, it is often placed on a turntable in the center of the table so that people sitting around the table can rotate the plate and select the food they wish to eat. When applied to customer service, the rotating plate is the method or system, and the food is the menu of needed or helpful ideas to be selected and employed by the company.

3. **And allowed to permeate.** This is a key facet of the infusion pump approach. Just as medication from an infusion pump is consumed and transported to every part of a patient's body, the goal in providing excellent customer service is to allow an "attitude of customer service" to penetrate and flow into every nook and cranny of the business. It must be an enterprise-wide experience – where beneficial changes permeate every muscle, fiber, and cell of the organizational being.

4. **In a controlled manner.** This statement implies that the process of change from a non customer-centric business to one that is truly customer-centric does not happen over night. It is not like turning on a light switch. Rather, it is a steady process of focused change over a period of months and years. Why? Because just as a cruise ship can't turn on a dime, neither can most businesses – and because it takes time for customer attitudes to change and for them to see, understand, and embrace the changes that are being made in the organization.

5. **In order to effect permanent, positive change**. The goal in doing all of this is not to create yet another "flavor of the month". We want permanent, positive change that will forever impact the way we run our businesses.

6. **Create greater well being, growth, and profitability**. If you do the job properly, this is the harvest you will reap for years to come. This approach creates happy, engaged employees, delighted customers, and ultimately helps to solidify the presence of your business in the markets you serve.

So – armed with an understanding of **The Customer Conundrum**, **Your Customers**, and **The Infusion Pump Approach**, we are now ready to look at some examples that demonstrate the entire range of customer service as it exists in our world.

PART TWO

THE UGLY, THE BAD, AND THE EXCELLENT

Why are these juxtaposed to The Good, The Bad, And The Ugly? Because we are on a journey to create outstanding customer service!

CHAPTER FOUR
Ugly Customer Service Destroys Companies

The T-Mobile Debacle

Almost two years ago, my family and I began searching for a new, more affordable cell phone plan. At the time, T-Mobile had one of the best offers, and we received an additional discount through my daughter's employer. Bottom line, we were to receive unlimited talk, unlimited text, and 200 Mb of data per phone for 5 lines – for a total cost of $104.90 per month. I was flabbergasted at the pricing because we had been paying $160 per month with another carrier and had 1,000 minutes to share, unlimited text, and only data on one phone. I was so shocked, in fact, that I actually printed the details from T-Mobile's website and asked customer service several times to verify that the offer was true.

Needles to say, we placed the order, committed to a 24 month contract, and anxiously awaited the arrival of our SIM cards. We got a very rude awakening when they arrived. Here's the comparison:

Promised: Unlimited talk on all 5 lines.
Actual: Unlimited talk on 1 line, 250 minutes per month on each of the remaining four lines.

Promised: Unlimited text on all 5 lines.
Actual: Unlimited text on all 5 lines.

Promised: 200 Mb each of data for all 5 lines.
Actual: 200 Mb of data on 2 lines; no data on the remaining 3 lines.

Now here's where things start to get really interesting. I called customer service to get things straightened out. After talking to several people and being escalated to a call center manager, I was told that the only recourse that I had was to contact T-Mobile Corporate Customer Service,　because the call center could not override the system and make the changes I was requesting, even though they completely agreed with my position and what I should have received. The only issue? T-Mobile Corporate Customer

Service is located at a P.O. Box in Albuquerque, New Mexico. They have no street address, no telephone number, and no fax number. (Gee – I wonder why?)

I assembled all of the documentation to prove my point, along with a detailed cover letter explaining, blow-by-blow, what I was promised and what I expected to get, and mailed the entire package (20+ pages) to customer service at a cost of about $6 (certified mail, return receipt). What happened? Nothing. Absolutely nothing.

Over the period of the next six months, I repeated this process five times, all to no avail. Since this approach wasn't working, and because every time I contacted regular customer service they said there was nothing they could do, I began digging and finally found a fax number at T-Mobile's corporate offices in Bellevue, Washington. I began faxing all 20 pages to them once a week, without fail. Finally, at long last, after 15 months, I received a letter saying that they would credit my account $250. No apology. No, "We're sorry. What can we do to make it right?" And even though I've tried to contact them ever since, I have gotten not one response.

Bottom line, our contract is up this coming December. I don't care if I have to pay more for my cell phone service. I will switch carriers because I refuse to tolerate this level of incompetent customer service.

Fast Food Fiasco
Submitted by Donna Mason, Owner of Summer Enterprises

Our horrifying customer service experience definitely took my husband, our 8-year old son, and me by surprise. It was so impactful that my son still talks about it nearly every day.

A couple of weeks ago, the three of us decided to go to the drive-in to see a movie. On the way, we planned to go through the McDonald's drive-thru to surprise my son with a Happy Meal. When we pulled into the parking lot, the drive-thru line was long and getting longer. On top of that, none of the cars were moving. We thought about pulling out of the line and forgetting the Happy Meal, but the line finally started moving, so we stuck it out.

My husband ordered a plain cheeseburger Happy Meal for a boy. When we finally arrived at the pick-up window, there was an older woman there who was yelling at the employees behind her at the top of her lungs. As she handed the bag to my husband, he politely asked if it was a plain cheeseburger. The woman glared at him and said, "Give me the bag!" She proceeded to dig in the bag, grab the burger, peel back the wrapping paper, and open it with her filthy, ungloved hands. It was the wrong burger, so she turned to the employees, cursed at them, and told them that the order was all wrong and that if they didn't start getting things right, they were all fired. My son heard her swearing, as did everyone in the restaurant, that was packed with patrons at the time.

My husband, who is not normally at a loss for words, was taken back by this behavior and didn't know what to say. We waited patiently for what seemed like an eternity and the lady finally gave us the "right" meal. No apology for the mistake or the extra wait time – just a mean scowl.

I handed the bag to my son. When he opened it, the fries were stone cold and the bag contained a toy for a girl, not a boy. That was all it took for my husband to park the car and walk into the store.

When he got to the counter, my husband was greeted by a sweet young girl who immediately took care of the problem and got my son fresh, hot food – and the right toy. My husband asked the girl if the grumpy, swearing lady was her boss and she whispered, "Yes." He said that he felt so sorry for her having to put up with that kind of treatment.

Because of that experience, we will never go to that store again, and McDonald's reputation has been forever marred in our minds.

Key Takeaways:

Customer service departments must be empowered. Let's face it, nobody wants to spend 45 minutes on hold, and another 15 minutes explaining their problem, just to be told, "There is nothing we can do for you." If you can't trust your customer service people to make the right decisions and do the right thing for your customers and your business, then either something is wrong with you, or something is wrong with them.

Customer service must be the light on the hill and not hidden under a bushel. A customer service department that hides behind a P.O. Box with no listed telephone, fax, or email contact information is, in my humble opinion, completely worthless. To me, they are an excuse for a company that is neither honest nor interested in delivering what they promise.

Customer service must be from the top down. The business leader sets both the tone and pace of customer service. If the boss has no respect for the customer, then neither will the employees.

A customer-centric business is an employee-centric business. You cannot expect your employees to render good customer service until they know that you (a) care about them and (b) are engaged in service to them.

CHAPTER FIVE

Bad Customer Service Costs You Business

The Restaurant Chain vs. The Local Diner

As a business and personal coach, I spend a good deal of one-on-one time with my clients, both face-to-face and on videoconferences. When I am meeting a client who is nearby, we often get together at a local restaurant where we can talk quietly and share a cup of coffee.

I also chair a local businessman's group, and we have breakfast meetings every two weeks. We discuss a number of business related subjects and enjoy fellowship around the table.

For a number of months, I was using a chain restaurant in our town. They had a nice room in the back that offered a quiet atmosphere and privacy. I approached the restaurant manager about using it, and he was amenable to giving me access to it for both coaching and business meetings. He did so on the basis of the revenue that he would be generating (approximately $5,000 annually) and the fact that the room was vacant a high percentage of the time.

At first, things went well, but then there were some changes that caused problems.

1. The manager came to me and told me that, from that point forward, I would have to call in the day before I needed the room and make a reservation. He already had a schedule for the room that I had provided him, but he insisted that I call and make the reservation. It was, in my mind, an unnecessary inconvenience, but he would not budge.
2. On a number of occasions, even though I had called and reserved the room, I would arrive at the scheduled time to find out that the room was either not ready, or was   being used by someone else. When I asked the manager about it, he apologized and said it wouldn't happen again – but it continued to happen on a fairly frequent basis.

A few months later, a new client engaged me and suggested that we meet at a locally owned diner instead of the chain restaurant I had been using. It was further from my office, but I agreed to meet him there. The quality of the food and service at this diner was so impressive that I told them about my coaching business and that I also ran a local bi-weekly meeting of businessmen. I asked them if they'd be interested in my business and they said that they would love to "earn" my business. I gave them my schedule and informed my clients and associates about the change in venue.

When I arrived for my next meeting, they had a reserved sign on a table with my name on it. I asked if they needed any advanced notice (like the call-in requested by the chain restaurant manager) and they said that the schedule I had provided was more than enough.

I have been using this local diner for over six months now. Every time I go in, I am amazed by the caring service I receive. Everyone who works at the diner knows me by name, and they "earn" my business with each transaction. I would never think of going somewhere else. The large chain restaurant will never get my business again, and they lost $5,000 a year because of their lack of having a desire and commitment to "earn" my business.

The Energy Company
-Or-
Bait and Switch
Submitted by Niles Pierson, Owner of Paul Gregory's Restaurant
www.paulgregorys.com

Niles Pierson came out of a number of years in corporate America. He chose a location in town and, with his wife and brother, started a small restaurant, bakery, and catering business called Paul Gregory's. As a new business owner, one of the first steps Niles took in the community was to join the Chamber of Commerce. He wanted to support the community and be able to network and become associated with other local business owners.

Shortly after Niles joined the Chamber of Commerce, he was told about a way to save on his energy bills. The deregulation of energy in the state had created a burgeoning market for alternative sources of energy supply, and the Chamber was endorsing one particular company that was promising rates far below the standard utility company prices. Niles investigated the company, believed them to be legitimate, and signed up.

At first, things seemed to go well, and Niles was saving on his utility bills. However, without notice, the rates began to increase and, at one point, ballooned more than 200% and were more expensive than the standard utility rates. Niles eventually switched to another energy supplier, one who had his best interests at heart.

The Lost Heirloom
Submitted by Mary Ann Santacroce, Attorney and Owner of Santacroce Law
www.santacrocelaw.com

I spent a week at Water's Edge Spa and Resort with my daughter and her friend. We had a wonderful week and generally experienced very good service. We checked out and everything was very uneventful. When I arrived at home, I received a voicemail on my cell phone telling me that housekeeping had found a necklace that was left in our room. My daughter was thrilled because she didn't realize that she had forgotten to pack a valuable family heirloom. I was extremely impressed with the integrity of the housekeeping services. I called the resort and spoke with a very pleasant woman named Megan, who told me that they would be glad to hold the necklace until I returned a couple of weeks later. So far, no problems.

Two weeks later, we returned to the resort and, when checking in, I inquired about the necklace and explained what had happened. Unfortunately, I didn't recall Megan's name at the time. The check-in person was very pleasant but couldn't locate the necklace. She checked with the manager on duty who said she didn't know anything about it. I persisted (a little too strong for my daughter's taste) and the manager came out to talk to me.

Her response was, "If it isn't on my list, then it doesn't exist, since I'm the only one who would hold found items." Needless to say, that didn't sit well with me. I asked her if she was saying that I was making this story up or if she was telling me that they lost the necklace? Either way, I told her in no uncertain terms that her attitude and misplacing the necklace were both totally unacceptable. She just responded by saying there was nothing she could do. After my refusing to take no for an answer, she did say she would check with someone else who might've been on when this took place and agreed to call me if she learned anything. (I think she only did this as a ploy to get me out of the lobby). Throughout this conversation, the check-in clerk remained entirely composed, friendly, and even apologetic.

Later that afternoon, I found the voicemail on my phone with the detailed information that I had received from Megan. I called to speak with the manager to give her the information and she seemed aggravated that I was calling her back and interrupting her. As it turned out, Megan was coming to work shortly and the manager agreed to check with her when she got in. When I returned to the front desk, Megan was there and introduced herself. She said, "I'm the one who called you. I have your necklace locked in a secure drawer. It looked valuable and I wanted to make sure it was kept safe. I'm really sorry that no one thought to look there."

All ended well, but I couldn't help but think the manager should have apologized, not Megan. That never happened.

Sales And The Fish Pond
Submitted by Lauren White, Community Relations Coordinator at PayHub
www.yourpayhub.com

I work in small business sales. Every week, I meet with all types of business owners and personalities. The variety of businesses run the gamut, from auto body shops to dental offices.

Recently, I had an appointment scheduled with a garden center. I must preface my comments by saying that the owner of the business is known for having wonderful products, but notorious for providing sub-par customer service.

I arrived right on time for my meeting, but the owner had completely forgotten about it. He was leaving the building as I was entering, but he was not apologetic, nor did he even take a moment to speak with me. He just asked me to reschedule and then left. I was happy to reschedule and arranged another appointment with his office manager.

While in the building, I noticed that the phone was ringing, but no one was making a move to answer it. This was disconcerting to me, because I am (or was) one of his clients.

As a client, I called him later that week to make an appointment for him to service my Koi fish pond. (His company is the only one in town who offers this service.) They did not arrive on the scheduled date and time. It was a no show accompanied by no call to let me know that they weren't coming. I followed up that evening, but when I called I only got voicemail. They finally arrived two weeks later to clean my pond. On top of that, it took them four months to send me an invoice for the work.

The two major issues I had with this company were lack of communication and timeliness. If they ran into a problem and needed to reschedule my appointment, I would have understood. But I think that I at least deserved a phone call to let me know what was going on.

I am now a former customer. I hired a company fifteen miles away to take care of my pond. They arrive on time, do good quality work, and they communicate with me about the work they are doing.

So what can we learn from these three stories?

Business must be earned and never taken for granted. Just because I do business with you today is no indication that I will do so tomorrow.

Earning is a present tense word indicating ongoing action. When we talk about earning someone's business, we can never look at it as "one and done". Earning is an ongoing process – something that we must do with every customer interaction.

Never take the customer for granted. Taking your customers for granted is the beginning of the slippery slope toward failure. It leads to a lackadaisical attitude, and that attitude eventually leads to apathy. When you don't care about your customers, you have no reason to expect them to care about you and continue doing business with you.

Meet your commitments. I don't know how many times I have heard business people say that the reason they landed a new customer is because they were the only ones who showed up. Meeting your commitments, like keeping appointments and doing the work you promise to do, are very simple actions that keep customers coming back for more.

The customer is always right. As business owners, we need to be about solving problems, not assigning blame. Trying to convince someone they're wrong is a futile game to play, and it does nothing to address the issue and build good will.

Stu Leonard, owner of the grocery store chain that bears his name, once had a sign hanging prominently in his Norwalk, Connecticut store. The sign said:

Stu's Rules

Rule #1: The Customer is ALWAYS right!

Rule #2: If you ever think the customer is wrong, read Rule #1 again!

CHAPTER SIX
Excellent & Getting Better Every Day

Some companies seem to have customer service down pat from the very beginning. They treat their customers well and, as a result, they garner tremendous followings no matter where they go. Here are a few great examples.

Apple Computer

Several years ago, I had the misfortune of dropping my iPhone on the ground and shattering the screen. It was my own fault, and admittedly a very stupid move on my part. I returned home late one night from a business trip. I had stopped along the way to take a phone call, and on completion of the call, I had put the phone in my lap, rather than putting it back in the console. As I approached home, I was anxious to see my wife and tell her about the events of the day, so I pulled into the driveway and quickly got out of the car, not thinking or recalling that my phone was still on my lap. So – you guessed it – the phone tumbled to the ground, landed at precisely the right angle, and – pop!! – a screen that looked like a broken mirror.

Once in the house, I got online, made an appointment at my local Apple store for the next morning, and went to bed, all the while chastising myself for my stupidity and realizing that it was probably going to cost me $150 to get my phone fixed.

The next morning, I arrived a few minutes early for my appointment at the Apple store. I signed in, waited patiently, and was taken within a couple of minutes of my scheduled time. "Nice," I thought. "Good customer service so far." But I was not prepared for what happened next.

When I was called up to the Genius Bar (Apple's version of technical support), the young man there greeted me with a smile and asked for my Apple ID email address. He quickly pulled up my account on his computer and asked me what he could do to help me. When I showed him my phone, he chuckled and said, "Yup, we see quite a few of those." When I asked why, he explained that the glass on the iPhone screens is thin and has a lot of built in stresses introduced during the manufacturing process. As a result, if the screen gets hit with the right force at the correct angle, the glass shatters.

He asked me to give him a minute and he disappeared into the back room. When he returned, he had a box containing a brand new iPhone. I looked at him quizzically and said, "So you can't repair it? I have to buy a brand new phone?"

"No," he responded. "I can't fix it, but you don't have to buy a new phone. This one's on us."

I must have sounded incredulous when I said, "You're going to give me a new phone, even though it was my fault that my old phone broke?"

"Yup," was his reply. "You're a loyal Apple customer, and we take care of our customers."

I asked if he had gone to the back room to ask his boss for permission to give me the new phone. He said that he didn't need his boss's approval for such matters – that the decision was entirely his. He then took my old phone, transferred all of my data to my new phone, and five minutes later I walked out of the store a very satisfied customer.

Important lessons to learn from this experience:

1. Apple keeps track of what their customers buy. Having a history of purchases gives them information that helps when making customer service decisions.
2. Apple employees are not just trained. They are empowered to make decisions. As a result, you get better, faster customer service because they move quickly and have respect for your time.
3. While Apple products are generally more expensive than the competition, their reputation for excellent customer service, and for standing behind their products, makes consumers more than willing to pay more money.

Bozzuto Management Company

Bozzuto may not yet be a household name, but they are on the fast track to getting there, especially in the eyes of east coast apartment dwellers. Bozzuto's owns and manages a number of high-end apartment complexes from Boston to Washington, D.C. They own and manage some properties, but they also manage properties that are owned by others.

My first experience with Bozzuto was when my middle daughter lived in one of their properties in New Haven, Connecticut for two years. The facility was immaculately maintained, the maintenance staff was friendly and extremely responsive if any problems arose, and the concierge staff was pleasant, professional, and knowledgeable. Even when there was a gap of several months between visits to my daughter's apartment, the people there knew me by name and let me know that they were looking out for my daughter. They appreciated the concerns of a father with a young, single daughter living in the city.

I thought that we had just been lucky in the selection of this particular property and management company, until my two younger daughters moved into another Bozzuto property in downtown Boston. It was then that I began to realize that there was something special about this company. The same culture we had experienced in New Haven was clearly present in the staff at the Boston property.

The icing on the cake for me, however, came when my oldest daughter moved to Boston. She looked at a number of properties just outside the city and selected a Bozzuto property called The Atmark in Cambridge, Massachusetts. Once again, I was pleasantly surprised to see the "Bozzuto culture" at work at this location.

Shortly after my daughter moved into her apartment in Cambridge, I had the opportunity to speak with the property manager. I told her that this was our third Bozzuto property, and relayed our positive experiences to her. She took me by surprise when she said that the Bozzuto culture comes directly from their CEO. There is a certain type of personality that they look for when staffing their facilities. She told me a quote from the CEO that will stick with me for as long as I live:

"Hire the personality, not the resume."

She explained to me that almost every company hires a resume – but that they fire a personality. Culture is important in the hospitality and property management business. You can often train people and equip them with the skills to do the jobs they've been hired for, but you can't change their personalities – their attitudes and approaches to people and how to best serve them.

Farmington Bank

I recently had a need to set up a business checking account. My family and I have had our personal accounts at Farmington Bank for a number of years, so I went online to check out their business accounts. I was pleasantly surprised to find out that their business accounts are completely free, with no minimum balance requirements.

Since we do almost all of our banking online, it had been quite a while since I had visited the local branch, but it is close by, so I popped in the car and took a quick ride.

When I entered the branch, the branch manager greeted me. We had met on a few occasions, but I was surprised that she remembered my name. I told her that I wanted to set up a business account and fully expected her to introduce me to one of her employees. To my surprise, she said that she could handle that for me. She found my company online, quickly set up my account, took care of the initial deposit, and gave me all of the details and copies of my paperwork.

What happened next surprised me. She told me that I would never pay for checks and that there would never be any overdraft or late fees on my account. She then gave me all of her contact information – business and personal – and told me to call her 24/7 if I had any questions or problems, and that she would deal with them personally and immediately. I've only had to call her twice, but she has been true to her word.

The Exterminator
Submitted by Jared Percyz, DDS
www.southingtondentists.com

I have a new baby at home and became concerned one weekend when I noticed several wasps flying around inside the house. I became concerned that there might be more of them, so I contacted Jeff DeBishop, a local exterminator.

Even though it was a weekend, Jeff came right out and quickly identified the problem. There was a small crack between one of my windows and the adjoining masonry that had allowed the bees to get into the house and build a nest.

Jeff got his equipment and killed all of the bees, but in the process, he made a mess on the window. He assured me that he would be back to take care of it.

Jeff was more than good to his word. He came back the next day and thoroughly cleaned the window. But in addition, he took the time to mix a small amount of mortar and repair the crack where the bees had gotten in.

That's what I call customer service!

I think these four examples of customer service excellence should be in every management textbook used in every business and MBA program in the country. Why? Because they contain the very essence of what outstanding customer service is all about. Here is my summation of what we can learn from these four excellent organizations:

1. *Know your customer*. There is no substitute for knowing your customer, by name and by their buying habits with your company.
2. *Respect your customer's time*. Our lives are all overflowing with things to do. Those who respect our time and have streamlined their processes to make doing business with them seamless and easy will win more of our business.

3. ***Develop a culture of "high touch".*** We live in a world that can be very impersonal due to the level of technology. I had Sharifah Hardie, a premier online marketing expert, as a guest on my radio show. She explained the need for high touch in our society. She said, "Do you realize that I can sit in my home and, via the Internet, order virtually everything I need to live? I can buy furniture, clothing, groceries, movies, music – and all without having any contact whatsoever with a human being." We all crave human contact, and as business people, the more pleasant we can make that contact, the more people will like us, appreciate us, and give us their business.

4. ***Commit yourself and your business to constant and never ending improvement.*** In the online, global world that we live in, there are more and more people and businesses that are vying for the attention of **your** customers. You must always be one step ahead – and that is what this book is all about!

5. ***Always do more than you promise.*** Going above and beyond, even in small ways, earns you a tremendous amount of good will with your customers. Those who take the time to deliver more generate a loyal following and get more business, both directly and via referrals, than their competitors.

PART THREE

THE FRONT END OF YOUR BUSINESS

Getting Back to Basics

CHAPTER SEVEN
Introduction To The Optech's Model

It was the spring of 1989. I had just taken over as head of engineering for a large medical products manufacturing company. As I analyzed the capabilities of my new organization, the obvious technical strengths emerged. What I wasn't prepared for was the overall lack of business knowledge and acumen in the group.

Many organizations have created a tower mentality – an approach that confines people's thinking to one narrow specialty and keeps them from understanding how the puzzle pieces of what they do fit into, compliment, and complete the overall enterprise. It was because of this tower thinking that I created what has become known as the Optech's Model.

Prior to 1998, the model was just an informal tool that I used to teach the basics of business – primarily to technical, non-business people. When I started my own business, Optimum Performance Technologies, in 1998, this model became the cornerstone of my work and I named it *"The Optech's Model"* after my company (O = Optimum; p= Performance; techs = Technologies).

Since 1998, I've discovered that The Optech's Model has a wide range of uses, and I have always found it to be a great, and very robust, tool for both understanding businesses and ferreting out the root causes of many business problems.

Recently, I found a new application for the model. In late May, I met Colleen Ferrary, the head of Small Business CT (www.smallbusinessct.com), as a result of a post she made on a LinkedIn business group. I responded to her post, and the rest, as they say, is history. Our conversation went from corresponding on LinkedIn, to business emails, to an hour-long phone conversation on June 3rd, and finally to a face-to-face meeting at Tisane's in Hartford, Connecticut on the afternoon of June 12th.

As Colleen and I talked that afternoon at Tisane's, I was impressed with her fire and dedication for providing both educational and consultative resources to help grow small businesses in Connecticut. I was also pleasantly surprised when she told me about a seminar that Small Business CT was sponsoring in October, and I was humbled when she asked if I would be a keynote speaker at the conference and address the subject of customer service. I readily agreed, and my mind began working on both the subject and my approach as I made the thirty-minute drive home from our meeting.

My mind was whirring with activity when I reached my office, and I sent a quick email to Colleen thanking her for the opportunity to speak at the conference, announcing that the title of my talk would be **The Customer Conundrum**, and that the same title would be emblazoned on the cover of a new book I was going to write for release on the day of the conference. This is the book you now hold in your hands.

For the next several weeks, I continued to ponder, pray, brainstorm, do research, and make notes about this new writing venture to which I had committed myself. As I thought through all of the customer service issues I had encountered and dealt with over the years, it became clear to me that this was yet another arena where The Optech's Model could be very effectively applied. I immediately engaged Joseph Cekauskas, owner of JC Marketing Communications (www.jcmcom.com) to help with ideas concerning the cover design of the book, and to help me create a more compelling, visually appealing version of The Optech's Model – a challenge to which he brilliantly arose, I might add.

So at this point, you are probably salivating and wondering – what the heck is The Optech's Model and what makes it so special?

I think that the key to The Optech's Model is in the simultaneous simplicity – and yet the profound depth and wisdom – that it offers. It is simple enough that a ten year old can grasp it, yet profound enough that the CEO's of some very successful businesses have, and continue to use it as a powerful problem-solving tool in their organizations.

The Optech's model is divided into three sections. Section One is **The Front End of Your Business**. It deals with the basics of producing your unique products and services. Section Two is **Looking Behind The Curtain**. It addresses all of the behind the scenes activities in your business – what some people call the "back room". And finally, Section Three is **Your Most Valuable Resource**. It is the one critical key that will allow your business to succeed against seemingly insurmountable odds.

This 9-faceted model, with a solid gold core, holds "the keys to the kingdom" of your future success as a business – so turn the page and let's get into the details!!

CHAPTER EIGHT

The Golden Core

$$G = \$$$

At the core of The Optech's Model is an oval containing the equation $G = \$$. In a moment, I'll explain this, but first let me ask you a critical question. If I asked you to define what a business is, could you? By that, I mean could you give me a really solid definition of what a business is?

Most people define a business as an organization that sells products or services at a profit. That's a pretty good general definition, but is it good enough?

Let me give you my definition of a business:

A business is a repeatable, duplicatable process that:

1. **Creates and delivers something of value.** If you are not offering a product or service that provides value, you are finished before you start. This may seem obvious, but you would be surprised at the number of people who have ideas for products or services that they are very excited about, yet these products or services bring no value to the marketplace.

2. **That other people want or need.** In addition to delivering value, your product or service must be something that others need or want. This statement serves to filter out some of the ideas from #1 above, because creating value that does not satisfy a need or want in the marketplace is futile.

3. **At a price they are willing to pay.** Every product or service has a price point. That point is the upper limit of what people are willing to pay. If you are below that point, enough people will potentially buy your product to enable you to generate decent sales. If you are above that point, the number of people willing to purchase your product or service declines significantly.

4. **In a way that satisfies customer's needs and expectations**. You can create value and provide a product or service that people want, and at a price they are willing to pay – but – are you meeting their needs and expectations? Every customer has ideas about what your product or service should do for him. Some of these ideas are based on your customer's specific needs, and some may be based on the product or service features that are already being provided by your competition. Customer needs are things that must be met. And, in addition, the more of their *expectations* you can meet, the easier it is for you to differentiate yourself from your competition.

5. **So that the business makes enough profit to make it worthwhile for you to stay in business**. In #3, we talked about price points. The market has a certain price that it is willing to pay for your product or service. The question to be addressed now is – are your costs to produce your product or service low enough to enable you to make a profit that is sufficient for you to stay in business?

Eli Goldratt, in his book **The Goal**, states that the goal (G) of every business is "to make money". In addition, he extends his statement to include "both now and in the future". So then:

The GOAL (G) of every business is to make money ($) both now and in the future (G=$).

Using the 5-step definition above gives you many of the key ingredients to make money today, and for many tomorrows.

Having said that, I am now about to make an emphatic statement that may seem like business heresy to you – and that is:

One does not make money by focusing on making money!

That's right. Listen to me carefully. Money is not a product. Money is a by-product – a by-product of the service you render to your **customers**. So the key to a successful business is to simultaneously appreciate money for the value (and necessity) it has for your business – but to make your customers, not money, the central focus of your business efforts. If your customers aren't happy, then they will go where they can find happiness – and that is in the arms of your competition. Without customers, you have no revenue, and without revenue you have no business. If you reach that point, money will be irrelevant – because you won't have any!

So now that we understand the primary goal of the business, and the need to focus on your customers in order to achieve that goal, the next four chapters will look, one point at a time, at the four initial facets for meeting the requirements we've defined in this chapter.

CHAPTER NINE
The Reality of Quality

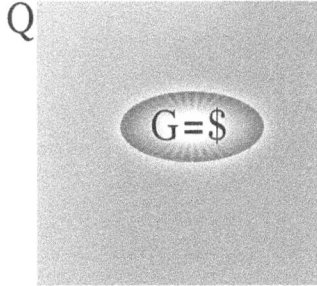

As we begin to extend the structure of the Optech's Model, we'll start in the upper left corner of the diagram and, in the next few chapters, we'll work our way in a clockwise direction until each corner of the square has been filled and identified.

In the upper corner, you now see the letter "Q". The Q stands for **Quality**.

What is quality? Do you really have a clear understanding of what it means in relationship to your business and your customers?

Think about the word and the various meanings it has in our lives:

- A *quality* product – means it is made of good materials
- *Quality* can also refer to reliability – a product that will last for many years
- *Quality* at your favorite restaurant can mean several things – impeccable service, cleanliness, the appeal of the atmosphere, and the preparation and presentation of the food and drinks being served
- When a product or service is rendered with an inordinate amount of attention to detail, we say that it is *high quality*

Take a few moments and make your own list of how you use the word *quality*, and in what places and contexts you apply it. Then try to create your own unique, all encompassing definition of quality.

It's not as easy as it seems, is it? *Quality* is one of those words where many of us have to admit that, "we know what it is when we see it or experience it, but it defies definition."

Let me take a stab at a definition that I believe fits nearly every, if not all, situations:

Quality is conformance to the requirements of the customer.

Pretty simple definition, isn't it? All we have to do is give the customer what he wants – what meets his requirements – and we have delivered a *quality* product or service.

However, this begs a second question. **How do we know what those requirements are?** Ah…now there's the rub!

Some customer requirements are relatively easy to determine. Earlier in the book, we discussed the widget that Company 'A" was manufacturing for Company "B". If Company "B" provided a blueprint, or other descriptive document, defining what the widget was to look like – and what dimensions and tolerances were to be met – then Company "A" has at least a basic understanding of the *customer requirements*. But does that mean that by providing a widget that meets those specifications, that Company "A" has *conformed to the requirements of the customer*? Maybe – and maybe not.

The point that I am trying to make here is that producing a quality product or service does not just involve some impersonal exchange of data (i.e., give me a blueprint and I'll give you a widget). It involves getting to know your customer.

There is a truism that reminds us that people do business with people – people they *know, like, and trust*. The first building block is getting to know your customer and letting him get to know you. The process must start with this and it must be initiated by you and your organization. It then must proceed in order of the words above. People can't like people they don't know, and they can't, and don't, trust people they don't like.

Why the emphasis on getting to know your customer? Because it allows you to build a relationship. But more importantly, it allows you to understand what your customer *needs*, not just what he's telling you he *wants*. I have encountered numerous situations in my business career where what the customer adamantly proclaimed he wanted had nothing at all to do with what he needed. Knowing your customer allows you to add value to his business by really nailing down and establishing, on both sides, the real requirements of the job to be performed.

Allow me to give you a good example. A number of years ago, I was working in a role where I was providing technical support for a sales organization. The company I worked for was selling industrial robots and related custom-designed automation. I got a call from one of our salesmen with a request to visit a customer with him. He was very excited because he believed that he had an opportunity to sell about six robots that, in combination with other automation, might yield a sale of around $300,000. The application was for material handling of extremely small shafts – drill blanks – into and out of grinding machines. I visited the company with the salesman to review the application and help in the preparation of a quotation and timeline for doing the work. The owner of the company was a really nice guy. He was convinced that robots were exactly what he needed, and he was prepared to make a substantial investment in order to be able to automatically load and unload his grinding machines. As we stood on his manufacturing floor observing employees loading and unloading machines, I told him that he didn't need robots to accomplish the task at hand. He vehemently disagreed with me until I took out a pad of paper and quickly sketched a simple mechanism that would accomplish the job at a fraction of the cost of a robot. The bottom line? The customer got what he **needed** – and saved $200,000 in capital expenditures. That is real quality!!

There is one other aspect of quality that I think we all need to understand. I read a while ago that **quality is no longer a competitive weapon**. The person who penned those words was trying to make the point that having world-class quality has become the price of entry into the marketplace, and that without it, you are doomed before you start. While I agree that a certain level of quality is necessary for entrance into the markets you serve, I disagree with the statement that quality is no longer a competitive weapon. In my experience, there are far too many companies whose definition and approach to quality is too narrow. If they would do the simple things I suggest in this chapter, and expand their quality efforts to embrace and really know their customers, then their quality would become so superior that it would decimate their competitors.

Remember, *Quality* is conforming to the requirements of your customer by knowing your customer and gaining agreement with him regarding what he really needs. Those who learn this valuable customer service lesson will succeed in circumstances where many others have failed

CHAPTER TEN

The Relationship of Cost And Profit

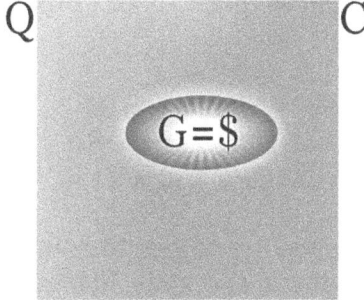

The next facet of the model brings us to the letter C – and you guessed it – C stands for **Cost.**

In Chapter Four, The Golden Core, we talked about the need for our businesses to be profitable. What is profit? Profit occurs when revenue exceeds expenses. That is a very macro definition of profit, but you get the point. We have to be bringing in more money on a daily, weekly, monthly, and yearly basis than we are spending if we wish to remain in business.

Over the past thirty years, the basic profit model has changed due to a combination of global competition and more informed consumers. When I graduated from college and started my first job in a manufacturing business, we used this model:

FAMC + P = SP

where

FAMC = Fully Absorbed Manufacturing Cost
P = Profit
SP = Selling Price

So in this model, we collect all of the costs associated with the manufacture of the product, add our desired profit margin, and arrive at the price we are going to charge the customer. Let's say that my manufacturing cost for a widget is $100 and I want to make a 30% profit on each widget. In this case:

$$FAMC + P = SP$$
$$\$100 + 30\% = SP$$
$$\$100 + \$30 = \$130$$

Unfortunately, as much as we might love to continue using this model, it is no longer valid in today's global economy. It has been replaced by another model.

$$SP - FAMC = P$$

where

$$SP = Selling\ Price$$
$$FAMC = Fully\ Absorbed\ Manufacturing\ Cost$$
$$P = Profit$$

You can easily see that both formulas contain the same elements. However, in the second formula, the elements have been re-arranged into a sequence that will, in many cases, produce dramatically different results. The new model says that Selling Price, minus the cost to manufacture the product, equals profit – and I might add a caveat here – "if any".

So what is driving this change? Price sensitivity in the market place. Products today have what is called a price point. That point is the maximum amount that a customer is willing to pay for a given product or service. Exceed that price, and your ability to sell your wares goes down dramatically. Stay under that price, and your chances of generating sales go up.

In the second formula, let's say that the price point (what the customer is willing to pay) is $100 and my manufacturing cost is $115. In this example:

$$SP - FAMC = P$$
$$\$100 - \$115 = (\$15)$$

The other factors that come into play here, again thanks to global competition, are how your price compares to that of your competition and how you have chosen to differentiate yourself in the market place (i.e., what value do you add, or what features do you offer, that your competition doesn't).

This part of the model is crucial because, in a global economy, labor costs and regulatory requirements vary greatly from country to country. Here are some suggestions for optimizing your costs and winning more business:

- Have a clear understanding of the costs associated with the production of your products and services
- Use statistical tools, like Pareto lists, to identify major cost drivers and to track trends
- Have an ongoing company-wide cost reduction effort to make sure that you are always identifying and capitalizing on opportunities to reduce costs
- Partner with your customers in joint efforts to improve and modify product designs for better manufacturing yields
- Invest in more robust, efficient equipment where it makes sense and where the payback is realistic
- Brainstorm how you can create and use differentiation in both products and services as a competitive weapon to beat your competition and increase customer followings and loyalty

How important is having a robust cost structure? Here's a great example.

I was working with a manufacturer of disposable medical devices when a foreign competitor engaged the company in battle. This competitor invested over one hundred million dollars to build a plant in the United States and, upon opening their doors to the American markets, they proudly announced that their primary goal was to achieve a 25% share of the market within 5 years. While the new entrant into the American market had a good product, they did not have the market presence or the sales and marketing capabilities of my employer. After two years, and with barely 1.5% market share, the competitor began a pricing war in a desperate attempt to gain market share by severely under bidding the price point. However, the competitor had not done his homework. The market price point was $0.25 per unit. The competitor's manufacturing cost was $0.10. What the competitor did not know what that my employer's fully loaded manufacturing cost was $0.035 – just 3.5 cents! This low manufacturing cost had been attained through years of constant product development and redesign, investing in and refining manufacturing technology, and strong and ongoing negotiations to keep the cost of materials and supplies at an absolute minimum.

The result? The competitor went out of business and closed his doors in less than five years.

Cost. A major tool in your arsenal to achieve customer satisfaction and gain market share.

CHAPTER ELEVEN
Timely Delivery

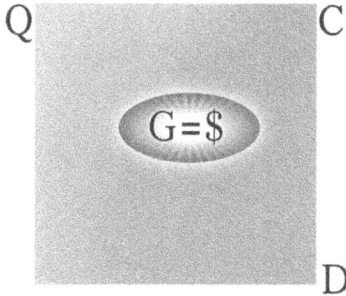

$$Q \qquad\qquad\qquad C$$
$$G=\$$$
$$D$$

OK. I've done it now. The title of the chapter gave it away. It's pretty clear that the D stands for delivery. It's obvious to every businessperson that delivery is important. The customer wants what he wants, when he wants it. What may not be so obvious are the implications of how we approach delivery.

Let me tell you another quick story. Several years ago, a manufacturer of durable medical equipment engaged me as a consultant. They were struggling with on time delivery (OTD) and had not been able to identify or correct the root causes of the problem. When I first visited them, they were quoting 4 to 6 weeks for product shipment, but actual shipment time was running in the 10 to 12 week range. This company was using a make-to-order model. They received an order from a customer, entered it into the production system, and if everything went according to plan, the customer would get a notice that his product was shipping in somewhere around 10 weeks. This was not a good scenario, and it yielded a lot of very angry customers!

It took a relatively short period of time – only a few days – to get to the root of the problem and begin fixing it. But what shocked me was what I discovered totally by accident. I was having lunch with the president of the company and just happened to ask him who his main competitor was. When he told me, I almost fell out of my chair. When he asked me why I was so shocked, I blurted out, "You're using the wrong business model!" He asked what I meant. I explained to him that his business was based on a make-to-order model, but the business model his competitor was using was make-to-stock. His competitor had an enormous advantage because he could deliver in one day – not 4 weeks.

Today, companies are falling all over themselves to get the best delivery. They offer free shipping for minimum purchase amounts; they upgrade shipping from ground to 2-day; they are even experimenting with using drones to deliver product. All for the sake of getting stuff into their customers hands quicker. Why? Because we live in an instant fulfillment society. We want what we want – **and we want it now**!

There are two distinct steps to remember when it comes to delivering your quality, cost-effective product or service:

1. Just as in the story above, your delivery model must be appropriate for the markets you serve, and in line with the timeframe being used by your key competitors.

2. You must have a system for making sure that you meet the commitments you make to your customers. If you say delivery in 4 weeks, then make sure that you hit that target 100% of the time.

Delivery completes the triad and is the culmination of the Quality – Cost – Delivery effort. These three elements represent the core of your business. They are the foundation upon which your business is built, whether you manufacture a product or offer a service. No business can survive without these three essential ingredients, so it is incumbent upon you to use them, both strategically and tactically, to serve your customers in ever better and more creative ways.

CHAPTER TWELVE
Demand & Sales

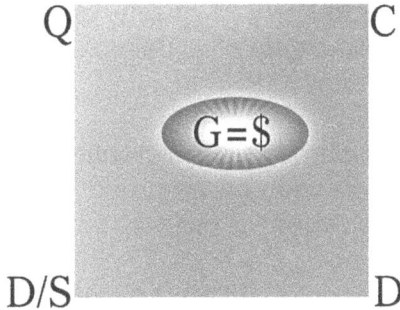

$$Q \quad\quad C$$

$$G=\$$$

$$D/S \quad\quad D$$

When you look at your business as a two-dimensional model, the result is what you see above. We've already discussed:

- **Quality** in which your product or service conforms to the require-ments of your customers
- **Costs** that allow you to simultaneously stay under the price point and make a profit that is sufficient to keep you in business
- **Delivery** that is 100% on time and competitive with others serving the same markets

Doing these things consistently and effectively sets the stage for the creation of **Demand**.

From this point forward, your sales and marketing teams are equipped with the basic tools to move your products into the marketplace with a far above average chance of generating **Sales**. In fact, if you have followed the guidance suggested thus far in this book, you should have some blossoming customer relationships that are already starting to produce fruit for you. You should also be starting to see that the system you are learning as a result of employing the Optech's Model really does work.

But there is a large problem here. Your business is not, in fact, two-dimensional. We live in a dynamic, full color, 3-D world – and there are other aspects of the model we need to explore in order to "bring all of the stars into alignment."

The next section of the book involves *Looking Behind The Curtain*. We are now going to peel back the layers of the onion and look at the key factors that make your business tick – the underlying mechanisms that either make the production and delivery of quality, cost-effective products and services seamless – or that create mountains and ravines that trip up you and your people at every turn.

You've begun an amazing journey toward creating a customer-centric business – a business of which you can be proud – and a business that will support you and your employees for years to come.

Turn the page, and let's continue our journey together.

PART FOUR

LOOKING BEHIND THE CURTAIN

What your customers don't see, but definitely feel, in your business

CHAPTER THIRTEEN
Systems & Processes

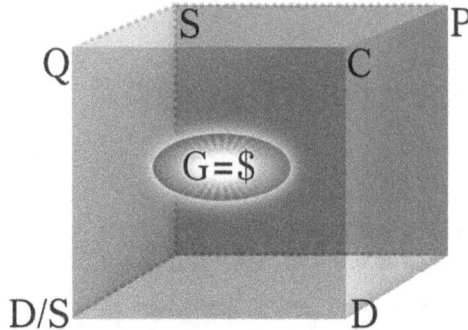

"Systems and processes have absolutely nothing to do with my customers, or with the level of customer service my organization provides!"

Those exact words came from the mouth of one of my clients when I suggested that it was not only appropriate, but necessary, to take a "peek behind the curtain" and look at the inner workings of his business from a customer service perspective.

I think that it is sometimes in our nature to look at our businesses as flat, two-dimensional entities. Our attitudes can often be just as that emphatically stated above. We may not be so vociferous in the way we state it, but the underlying tone is still there. Our thought process often is:

If I produce a good quality product or service, at a reasonable price, and deliver it on time – what has the customer got to complain about?

The subtitle of this book is, "9 Crucial Steps For Winning Customers And Outsmarting Your Competition". The first four – understanding your goal; producing a product or service that meets the requirements of your customer; doing so at a price point where (a) the customer is willing to pay the asking price and (b) your costs are low enough that you make a profit; and delivering that product or service quickly and efficiently – are the basic rules of playing the business game. Without them, you have no business and you cannot win any new customers or keep existing customers for very long.

Now listen to me carefully:

Successfully completing the first four steps in this process will allow you to begin winning new customers. But it's the last five steps that are the keys keeping those customers, getting more business and referral business from them, and outsmarting your competition in a way that leaves competitors so far behind you that they can't even see your dust!

The first step in our "peek behind the curtain" is to look at the Systems and Processes by which your business operates. In order to do this, let's first define what Systems and Processes are:

System: A collection of procedures, either formal or informal, written or verbal, that define how the various aspects of a business operate. Examples are the sales system, the finance system, the customer service system, and the production system.

Processes: A subset of systems that provide detailed instructions for how specific tasks are performed. Examples are the order entry process, the customer invoicing process, and the production scheduling process.

In some cases, the design of the various business systems and processes are controlled by regulatory agencies, as in the case of ISO (International Standards Organization), OSHA (Occupational Safety and Health Act), Sarbaines Oxley (financial management and reporting), and HIPAA (protection and sharing of medical information). In other cases, the systems are controlled by either company management or those actually doing the work.

The key questions you need to ask when dealing with systems and processes are:

- **How are they negatively impacting the quality, cost, and delivery of your products and services?**
- **How are they hindering your ability to delight your customers?**
- **How are they keeping you from outsmarting your competition?**

Every existing system and process needs to be reviewed with these three questions in mind, and then modified appropriately to be as streamlined, efficient, and customer-centric as possible. Also, a review process needs to be established so that all new and/or modifed systems and processes pass through this questioning process.

Depending on the size of your business, the tasks associated with reviewing and updating your systems and processes can be daunting, but the effort expended to achieve both major financial and strategic advantages is almost always very well worth it and pays tremendous dividends. In addition to pleasing your customers and creating dismay in the heart of your competition, here are some key benefits you'll reap:

- **An honest, open review of systems and processes always yields opportunities for improvement.**
- **It provides opportunities to document what you really do by involving those actually performing the tasks.**
- **It's a great training resource.**
- **It can become the springboard for a very effective continuous improvement process.**

One last recommendation. If you find yourself overhwelmed with this process, or if you're just having problems being really objective in your review and analysis, spend the time and money to find and hire a professional to help you. People like me, who have systems and process knowledge, combined with years of experience in a variety of industry segments, can provide a fresh, unbiased point of view, along with recommendations that provide returns far beyond the investment you will make.

CHAPTER FOURTEEN
Paradigms (No, it's not 20 cents)

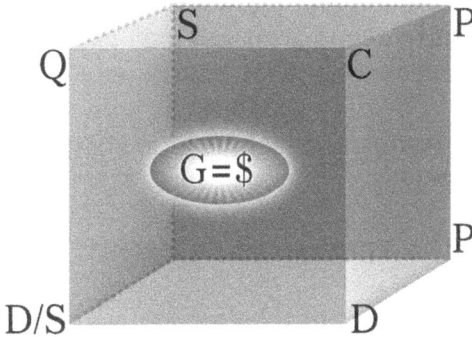

The word paradigm has become one of the most overused words in the English language. I wish I could come up with a fitting substitute, but alas, I can't.

Simply stated, **a paradigm is nothing more than the way we see our world, or our businesses, at any given point in time**. It is a snapshot of what we believe to be reality.

Paradigms are important for two reasons:

- If we are honest, and reasonably accurate in our assessments, they give us a good picture of today's reality.
- They encourage us to realize that today's reality – and the reality of tomorrow – may be very different things.

So what does this have to do with the subject of customer service? Well, let me ask you a couple of questions:

- **What do you see as the future of your business?** The status quo rarely remains the status quo for very long. The world is changing. Economic, geopolitical, and technological changes impact our businesses every day. Our ability to look into the future and create opportunities from these shifting sands is a major key to both the survival and success of our companies.

- **What do you see for the future of your customers?** If you are really a customer-centric business, do you not need to be a student of your customers wherever and whenever possible? Helping them identify paradigm shifts in their businesses and products can not only strengthen relationships and trust, but they can create many wonderful opportunities and synergies for both of your businesses.

Let me give you a few examples to highlight the importance of finding, and exploiting paradigm shifts.

The Shifting Watch Market

In the 1970's, the Swiss dominated the world's watch market. They had the best, most precise mechanical movements, and that led to accurate timepieces that could be passed from generation to generation.

However, by 1990, the Japanese had outsmarted their competition (the Swiss) and had captured the watch market with accurate, and much less expensive, watches. This resulted in a challenge to the Swiss economy as thousands of machinists and watchmakers lost their jobs due to the shrinking demand for their products.

So what happened? There was a fundamental paradigm shift that occurred in watch technology. It was a shift from the mechanical watch to the electronic watch. The Japanese saw this paradigm shift coming and the Swiss did not – and that, as they say, is the way this particular cookie crumbled.

Now – I am a fan of the late Paul Harvey. I always loved the way he postured his news articles in a way that, in the end, gave one the underlying truth of the matter. In that spirit, I offer you the following:

What most people are not aware of is this rare fact:

The Swiss invented the electronic watch movement

That's right. The Swiss, not the Japanese, invented the electronic watch, but they failed to see the significance of what they had created. They missed the paradigm shift – and that mistake cost them dearly.

We could prognosticate for a long time on why this slip-up happened. We'll probably never know for sure, but it most likely was because the Swiss were stuck in their own paradigm about how they viewed the world and, as a result, they lost their dominant position in the watch market.

And now you know the rest of the story.

Multiple Paradigm Shifts In The Music Industry

Many of you who are reading this book have not been on planet earth as long as I have. Now in my early 60's, I have seen the development of many of the technologies that people take for granted today.

One of the most interesting developments has been in the music industry. As a young boy, I vividly remember the heavy glass-like 78-RPM records and the small 45-RPM's that contained single songs. I've seen the media of music transformed from these antiques, to the 33-1/3 vinyl records and reel-to-reel tapes, to 8-tracks, to cassettes, to CD's, and now to almost exclusively delivered digital media.

As technology has improved, these paradigm shifts have taken place year after year after year. But let me ask you:

How many of the manufacturing companies who produced the original 78-RPM records – or even the vinyl records back in the 1960's and 1970's – are still around?

Not many. Why? Because they missed the paradigm shifts caused by ever evolving and improving technology.

Oil Prognostication

In the early 1970's, there was a think tank group of people, called The Club of Rome, who published a white paper with their predictions about the future of the oil supply on planet earth. When the paper was published, they claimed that in forty years, the earth's oil resources would be completely exhausted.

Fast forward to the early 1990's, twenty years later. When asked if their prediction was holding true – if indeed the earth's oil reserves would be gone in 20 years – their response was a resounding NO! They now believed that the world's oil supply would last for another 90 years!

When asked why they had changed their forecast, here is what they said:

- The calculated oil supply in the 1970's report only took into consideration the oil reserves at a certain depth below the earth's surface. In the intervening 20 years, new technology had been developed to reach oil at greater depths, thereby doubling the available supply of this precious resource.
- The consumption of oil-based substances, like gasoline, had slowed. This was caused by the shift from carburation to fuel injection in motor vehicles that dramatically increased fuel economy.

So you see, dear reader, paradigm shifts are all around us, and it behooves us to keep an ear to the ground, and to be constantly looking for what comes next, both for us and the customers we serve.

CHAPTER FIFTEEN
Technology

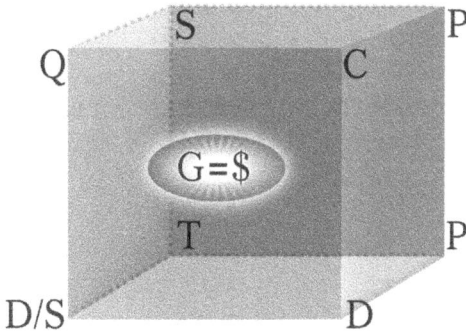

You may be wondering why this chapter is about technology when the last chapter on paradigm shifts discussed shifting technology and technological developments. The purpose of this chapter is to look at technology from a different perspective, and that is:

How does the technology in your business impact your customers?

Let me give you a great illustration:

This past May, my wife and I decided that we needed to replace the garage doors and automatic door openers in our home. I have become a real online shopper, so I went to the website of my favorite home improvement store and began looking. In short order, I was able to find a nice set of garage doors and place them in my shopping cart. Shortly after that, I selected two door openers and moved them to the cart. But when I went to purchase the installation, I hit a snag. I could purchase the installation, but there wasn't an adequate description of what the installation included. Was it just for a new install? Did I have to take down the old equipment or would they? Did I have to take the old stuff to the dump or was that included in the price? Because I couldn't get the answers, I couldn't complete the transaction and I had to plan a trip to the store.

When I arrived at the store, I was greeted by a friendly young man who asked if he could help me. I asked if he could point me to the garage doors and openers. To his credit he said, "Follow me. I'll take you back to the millwork department and introduce you to Ed. He's our resident expert on garage doors and openers."

By the time we got to the millwork department, this young man knew my name and exactly what I was looking for. He introduced me to Ed, told Ed what I needed, and left us to talk.

Ed asked me to sit down so he could get some information. I told him that I had already been online and knew what I wanted, so he asked me for my selections. I told him the size, manufacturer, and model I wanted for the garage doors. He immediately told me that I had made a bad selection, not because the doors were poor quality, but because he had just learned that the manufacturer was no longer offering warranty service in Connecticut. He helped me select another door of equal quality and saved me $200 because it was on sale.

Now onto the garage door openers. I had selected a ¾ horsepower opener. Ed said that I didn't need something that large. He said a ½ horsepower was fine and saved me another $300. Great individualized customer service thus far.

Then we sat down at Ed's computer to place the order and schedule the installation. At this point, I had been in the store less than 20 minutes. I was still there an hour later, as I went through the painful process of watching Ed enter the order and then get kicked off the system four separate times. He had what looked to be a brand new computer on his desk, so I asked him why he was having so much trouble. Ed explained that the computer was new, but that the software was fifteen years old and was riddled with flaws. He continued to explain that he, and other store employees, had brought this to the attention of both local and corporate management on numerous occasions, but they had been told that the company couldn't afford to upgrade the software.

Ed was visibly embarrassed and irritated as he related to me the number of customers who had left the store and done business with a competitor because they got tired of waiting to complete their purchases. He said that he had lost well over $100,000 in business in the last twelve months because of the stupid computer system. This company has hundreds of stores across the country that use the same software. The result is a loss of millions of dollars in revenue that could have been added to both their top and bottom lines.

In the story I just related, there are two examples of poor technology:

- A website that wouldn't let me complete what should have been a relatively simple transaction.
- A POS (Point of Sale) system that has outdated, unreliable software.

Lessons you can learn and benefit from concerning technology are:

- **Make sure that your website is designed from both a marketing and a customer service perspective**. Can visitors easily find what they are looking for? Is the necessary information there for them to make a buying decision without being overwhelmed with too much information? Is the checkout process seamless, secure, and easy?
- **Your POS system must be easy to use**. The goal is to allow customers to check out and get on with their lives, not to have them standing in long lines, or waiting for customer service to come to their terminal because an item is not recognized by the scanner, or the scanned price is incorrect.
- **Technology should make for a more pleasant transaction**. Those companies who realize this glean two benefits: more return customers and longer customer stays on their websites and in their stores.

PART FIVE

YOUR MOST VALUABLE RESOURCE & COMPETITIVE WEAPON

The Golden Key to Success

CHAPTER SIXTEEN

What Makes The World Go Around?

$$P = R + C$$

People = Relationships + Communication

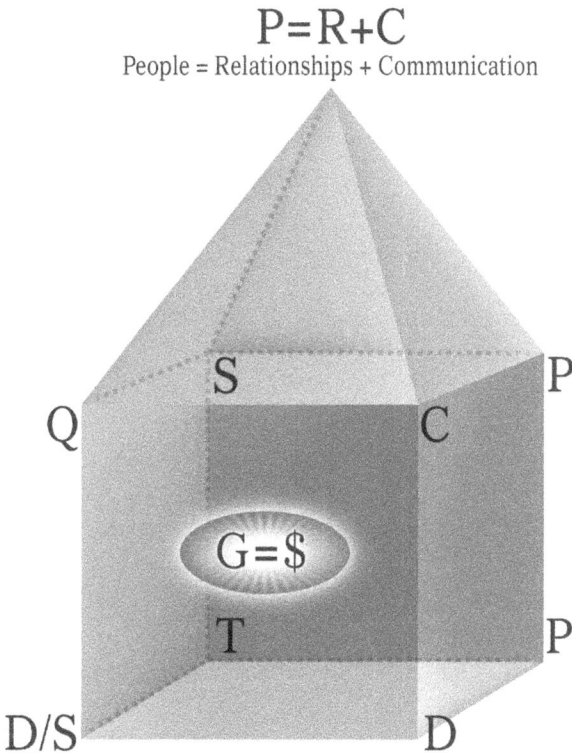

When I'm presenting the Optech's Model to audiences, I like this part of the program the most. At this point, we've covered the key elements that make up your business and we've discussed how each of them impacts your ability to simultaneously win customers, get more referral business from your existing customers, and strategically and tactically outsmart your competition.

Here's the question I ask next:

What makes it all happen?

Stop and think about it:
- Who makes a quality product or service?
- Who controls the costs?
- Who delivers your products?
- Who creates, monitors, refines, and improves your systems and processes?
- Who's looking out for future opportunities and protecting you from potentially dangerous paradigm shifts in your business?
- Who's developing and deploying the technology you use in your business, and teaching others to use it?

The answer is simple: **PEOPLE DO!!!**

But here's another conundrum for you. The answer is simple – but making it real in your business is not.

The equation above the peak of the pyramid is:

$$P = R + C$$
People = Relationships + Communication

Zig Ziglar said that you don't build a business. You build people – and people build the business.

I say it a bit differently:

The foundation of a customer-centric business is a people-centric business

In other words, you can't expect your employees to care for and serve your customers if you don't care for and serve them.

"Serve?" I can here the crashing thoughts in your mind as you glare at the page and say, "Serve? You're kidding, right?"

No, I'm not kidding. Serve is a simple word, yet it contains a richness and fullness in it's meaning – and it may just be the most important word in existence when it comes to building a successful business.

Learning to serve is one of the most difficult challenges many business owners and leaders face. Why? Because serving emanates from the heart, not the head.

Zig Ziglar had another saying that is very true:

You must BE before you can do, and you must do before you can have

Many people approach service to the customer (and to their employees) from a "do and then have" perspective. They completely ignore the BE part of Ziglar's quote – and they do so to their own peril and failure.

I created a quote that hits this topic head on:

You cannot consistently do that which you are not in your heart

Creating a customer-centric business involves three elements:

1. Developing a "servant's heart" and allowing it to permeate every fiber of your being.
2. Learning to serve your employees from the heart.
3. Teaching your employees to serve each other and your customers.

Developing the heart of a servant. As a business leader, it all starts with you. If you don't have a true servant's heart, you must change. This involves:

- Recognizing the need for change
- Making the commitment to change
- Developing a plan to change
- Implementing that plan

Learning to serve your employees. This is where the words from the formula, *Relationships and Communication* come in.

Employees want a meaningful connection with the business and, more importantly, with owners and leaders. I used to work as the engineering manager for a large manufacturing company. We had 250 people in the plant I worked in. One day, I was taking a walk on the manufacturing floor with the plant manager. Later that day when I was walking the production floor by myself, a number of people asked me who was that man that I was with earlier in the day. They had no idea who he was, because he almost never left his office.

As business owners and leaders, we need to spend time in the trenches. I love to work side-by-side with employees, assembling products, helping to set up machines, loading delivery trucks, and sweeping the floor. Why? Because it gives me a chance to get to know them and build *relationships*. When they find out that I'm just a regular guy and that I really am there to help them, they open up and all sorts of interesting things begin to happen that literally begin propelling the business forward.

The other operative word here is *communication*. You must have regular, meaningful communication with your employees. I support the philosophy of having an open-book business with monthly communications meetings involving all employees. You can choose how much to reveal in these meetings, but I've found it extremely beneficial when employees know:

- Is the company financially secure?
- How much are we selling, to whom, and what are the trends?
- Are we currently profitable?
- What challenges are the company facing and what is being done about them?
- Do we have any new customers? If so, who are they, what are we doing for them, and what does that mean for the future of the business?
- What are other departments, like Sales, Marketing, and R&D doing that is of interest?
- **How can they help?**

Teaching your employees to serve each other and the customer. Employees can't help each other and the customer unless and until they know where they fit in.

Here's a challenge for you. Go to each of your employees over the next few days and simply ask—

How does what you do every day effect your coworkers, our customers, and the business?

How many of them do you think can tell you without any hesitation? If your company is like most, the answer is – not many. And the answers you do get will usually be pretty lame.

This may be a bitter pill to swallow, but if your people can't answer this simple question, their inability to do so is your fault.

Along with relationships and communication comes another word: *Education.* There must be an ongoing education process that teaches em-ployees about your business in a way that connects them to you, each other, and your customers. The service that begins in your heart, must radiate outward and become absorbed by them. Then they must be taught how to pass it on. *Virtually every employee has some level of impact on the quality of service you provide to your customers.*

Here is the bottom line:

When you develop the heart of a servant
  When you begin serving your employees from that heart
    When you teach your employees to serve each other and the customer
      When your employees are fully engaged in the business

Then the heart and attitude of customer service will permeate your business like a sweet perfume, and you will begin to prosper in ways that you cannot begin to imagine.

CHAPTER SEVENTEEN

Negotiating and the Customer-Centric Business

When it comes to talking about customer service and building a customer-centric business, one of the topics most people shy away from is that of negotiating. People don't like to negotiate, and they see negotiating as something that stands in stark contrast, a polar opposite, to building a customer-centric business. I think the reason most people tend to have these feelings is because, deep down inside, they think that having a customer-centric business means that they become a door mat and allow the customer to walk all over them – **when nothing could be further from the truth**.

Whether we want to believe it or not, we are all negotiators. Every time you are nose-to-nose and toe-to-toe with another human being, chances are that you are negotiating. As a business owner, stop and think about all of the circumstances in which you find yourself negotiating:

- Coming to agreement with a new customer on the details, terms, and conditions of a purchase order
- Finalizing an annual supply agreement with one of your vendors
- Working with your Board of Directors or management team to determine compensation policies
- Coming to agreement on the content and wording of a union contract
- Settling a dispute between two employees

Even in our personal lives, we are negotiating all of the time:

- You and your wife are going out to dinner. She wants Italian and you want seafood.
- Your teenage daughter wants to go to a party, but you're not sure that you approve.
- You're having a family night at home to watch movies. Will you watch a chick-flick or an action movie?

So if we're really negotiating all of the time, why is it that most of us don't like it – and even more troubling – why most of us aren't any good at it?

I think that there are two reasons that most people don't like negotiating. The following two statements are also why a lot of negotiations start going sideways, and why a good number of them fail.

1. **We see negotiating as a win-lose proposition**. Somehow we have indelibly burned this into our minds. If you and I are negotiating about something, if I win, that means you lose. In the example above, my wife and I are going out to dinner. She wants Italian and I want seafood. So if I get my way and we go to a seafood restaurant, she loses? So you're telling me that Italian restaurants don't serve seafood? You get the point.
2. **People tend to negotiate sequentially rather than holistically**. In most negotiations, people have a list of issues that they are working through – those things that need to be resolved or agreed upon before the negotiation can be successfully concluded. I don't know how many times I've talked to people in the midst of a negotiation and they have told me, "We're almost there. We have only one issue left to discuss and we're not that far apart." Those are dangerous words. Why? Because when you are only negotiating on one point, it almost always comes down to a place where someone has to win and someone has to lose.

So what are we to do with this additional *conundrum* that I've just thrown into our laps? Let me give you an illustration that will help you to begin looking at things from an entirely different perspective.

First, imagine that you and I are sitting across the table from each other. I extend my hand to you palm forward, just like a police officer would do to stop traffic. I ask you to give me a detailed description of what my hand looks like, and after you have done that, I give you a description of what my hand looks like.

Are the two explanations given going to be the same? NO! They are going to be different. I might then ask you, "But it's the same hand. Which one of us is right?"

The answer is that both of us are right. The reason that our descriptions are different is that we are looking at the same object, but from two different perspectives.

You see, dear friends, when it comes to negotiating, it is our normal human tendency to make the judgment that we are right and the other person is wrong. We need to change the way we think in these circumstances and realize that, in any negotiation, both sides may be right but just looking at the same problem from a different perspective.

"But how does that help?" you ask. Well, if you realize that the other person is looking at the issue from a different perspective, should that not motivate you to try to understand what that perspective is? When you take the time to do this, you will often discover that what you both want from the negotiation is not mutually exclusive.

Almost universally, when we enter into a negotiation with someone else, we do so from the perspective of what we want – what we wish to get from the negotiation. But what if we also try to understand what the other person wants – and help him get it?

My thought process says:

If I know what you want and I help you get it, then the probability of my getting what I want increases dramatically.

I want to give you an excellent example that illustrates this point. Roger Dawson is known for being one of the world's greatest negotiators. He also teaches negotiating techniques and strategies. Roger spends a lot of time working with real estate investors, and he told the following story.

A real estate investor in Seattle, Washington, came across a piece of property that was an ideal site for building a shopping mall. He was excited to find this property and amazed that none of the other investors in the area had stumbled upon it. He assembled a group of business people who were willing to underwrite the project and he approached the owner of the property with an offer. To his surprise, his offer was met with complete indifference. The owner didn't say that the offer was good or bad – simply that he did not wish to discuss an offer on the land at that time.

Dismayed but still determined, the investor called Roger and asked for his assistance. Roger ignored the details given about the property and asked the man to tell him about the owner. The investor said that he didn't know too much about the landowner, but relayed the following to Roger:

- The owner was elderly, perhaps in his 80's.
- He was ill and knew that he had less than a year to live.
- He was very wealthy.

Roger surmised that the indifference the elderly man had shown to the investor's offer was because he didn't need the money. But then Roger began to think about what might motivate this elderly man to sell his land – in other words, what did the landowner want from this potential transaction?

Roger suggested to the investor that one thing this elderly man might be interested in would be leaving a legacy, and that perhaps offering to name the shopping mall after this gentleman might just do the trick.

When the investor met with the elderly landowner and told him about creating a legacy for him through the naming of the mall, the man signed over the title to the land to him, free and clear – the investor paid nothing for the land.

This chapter is not only a good opening to a course in negotiating – it has a strong tie to building a customer-centric business, because:

Customer focused businesses are based on the building of relationships in every aspect of your business. And when you have solid relationships in place, you know what the other person wants before the negotiations ever begin.

CHAPTER EIGHTEEN
Epilogue

A number of years ago, I knew a man who was amazingly successful in the multi-level marketing industry. He had a net worth approaching $50 million, and had built one of the largest MLM organizations in the world. For this story I'll simply call him "D".

Despite his success, D continued working his business because of the sheer joy he received from helping others become successful and achieve unusual amounts of financial prosperity.

One day, D met a gentleman who was a very wealthy stockbroker. He invited the man to attend a meeting where he could learn more and explore the possibilities of a new business venture. The man agreed and D said that he would pick him up that evening.

Right on schedule, D arrived at this man's beautiful home, picked him up, and started driving to the business meeting. The man, who was used to driving high-end automobiles like Jaguars and BMWs, was surprised that D was driving an old, and rather dilapidated pickup truck.

As they drove to the meeting, the stockbroker turned to D and said, "I have to tell you that going to a meeting in an old, beat up pickup truck is not very motivating."

D glanced at the stockbroker and replied, "I didn't buy it to motivate you. I bought it to motivate me." D went on to explain that there are two important keys that every super successful person learns:

1. **To be humble.**
2. **To never forget where you came from, and to go back and visit that place frequently.**

Why do I tell you this story as we close our time together? Because all of us, at one point in time or another, need to get back to the basics and go back and visit the humble places of our beginnings.

This book is not rocket science. It's all about focusing on the basics. There are many people out there who will tell you that you need a host of fancy equations and complex business models that only PhDs can interpret. I disagree. I think that the reason most businesses fail is because they lose sight of the basics.

A number of years ago, my oldest daughter decided to pursue the pathway toward becoming a physician. As part of the process, she was required to take the Medical College Admission Test (MCAT). She took it in the spring and, while she waited the nail biting three months to receive her test results, she worked in a lab at a local medical school. As it turned out, the head of the lab where my daughter worked was a Ph.D. He was planning to go to medical school and was also waiting for the results of his MCAT exam.

The day finally arrived and the test results were published. My daughter scored higher on her exam than the head of her lab did. Why? Was she more intelligent than he? NO! Was she any better prepared? NO! The reason his test score was lower was simply because he was so used to working at the Ph.D. level that he had forgotten most of his basic science. *He had not gotten back to basics in preparation for the test.*

Keep this book on your desk or bookshelf as a point of reference as you move forward. Use it to keep pulling you back to the basics as you build your own exciting, growing, profitable customer-centric business.

I hope that I get to meet you one day and hear your success story. I want to hear from you and learn how this book has benefited your journey. I'd also like your stories, ideas, and input to go into the next edition of The Customer Conundrum. You can always reach me at gary@optechs.com.

May God bless your journey, give you great success and, above all, may you live your life intentionally.

PART SIX

PRACTICAL APPLICATIONS

Putting the Optech's Model to Work

Top Down vs. Bottom Up

In this appendix, we will talk generally about Top Down vs. Bottom Up. My point in this section is that everything in your business starts with you, the owner or senior manager. Leadership that is going to change your business's approach to customer service must be top down – it simply can't be done from the bottom up.

So here is bullet list one:

- **It begins with leadership**. Leadership is the key, and leadership begins with you. Notice that I said leadership, not management. In his book, EntreLeadership, Dave Ramsey reminds us that any idiot can say, "I'm the boss and you're going to do as I say." Taking this approach is what is called positional leadership. Positional leadership means that I am higher on the food chain in this business than you are. Therefore, you are required to do my bidding and I don't have to explain why. The flip side of this coin is called persuasional leadership. Persuasional leadership says that I lead through relationships, communications, and by involving people. When you know how what you do fits into the grand scheme of things, it's easier for you to catch my vision and follow my lead.

- **Employees who are cared for care for customers**. Persuasional leadership leads to engaged employees – employees who are connected to and rooted in the business. They feel empowered and have a vested interest in growing the company. Therefore they strive to provide the highest levels of customer service.

- **No lip service allowed – only commitment**. Creating a customer-centric business is not a flavor of the month gig. You're either all in or all out. Make up your mind and move on. There is no room here for the wishy-washy Charlie Browns of the world.

- **Set the example**. If you're the leader, then leadership starts with the example you set. If you've screwed up in the past – admit it – to yourself and to your people. Heck, they already know it, so you're not revealing any deep, dark secrets. Come clean and be done with it! Make a commitment to change and ask your people to hold you accountable for doing so. They will help you and they'll love you for it.

- **Have a plan**. Work with your team to develop a plan. Take the time to analyze where your customer service efforts are falling short the most. Gather data and create Pareto lists. Here's a novel idea: talk to your customers! Prioritize the most impactful areas first, and then develop your plan with the help of your people.

- **Execute and report**. As you put your plan into action, notice what's working and what's not and make appropriate course corrections along the way. Report progress and challenges regularly to your entire organization, and ask for help in solving specific issues. Put teams together to look at specific problems and report back to you. And don't forget to do some teambuilding training first!

Following these guidelines will not only kick start your business – it will put you on the pathway to becoming an awesome leader.

APPENDIX TWO
Capitalizing On QCD

Quality, Cost, and Delivery are the three legs of a stool that are critical to every business. Without any one of them, the stool collapses and the business dies.

Here are some key things to consider regarding QCD:

- **Understand the requirements of your customer.** So many companies lose business and fail because they give the customer what he wants and not what he needs. Understanding customer requirements requires knowing your customer and his business. This requires a relationship between you and your customer, and that relationship, when properly forged, yields a goldmine of opportunities through which you can serve your customer and develop a mutually beneficial, long-term association that is profitable for both of you. And that is a huge win-win!

- **Produce quality products and services.** Once you understand the true requirements of your customer, make sure that that everyone associated with the production of the goods for this customer is aware of and focused on the critical goals. This is where your employees can use your systems and processes to capture details and plan an effective, efficient fulfillment process.

- **Control and continually reduce costs.** CANEI (Continuous And Never Ending Improvement) must become the mantra of your organization. Continuous means that the battle is never over. The goal is always reset and the bar raised higher.

- **Deliver your products on time.** This doesn't just mean meeting your commitments. It means understanding your target market and your competition. The ultimate goal in the delivery process is to be able to make, deliver, and get paid for your product before you have to pay for the materials used to produce it. How's that for positive cash flow?

- **Use QCD as a strategic weapon.** Harness the power of QCD to get more business from existing customers, give them the trust to refer you to other potential clients, and to confound your competition with world-class quality, reasonably priced, and instantly delivered.

APPENDIX THREE
Systems and Processes

The systems and processes areas of your business will almost certainly yield some very fertile ground for improving customer service. Why? Because rarely, if ever, do people think of internal systems and processes from the perspective of how they will enhance, or degrade, the experiences that customers have with their organizations.

Here are some illustrative examples:

* What are your procedures for forecasting customer demand? How often do you do it? Do you monitor forecasted vs. actual demand? Do you involve your customers in the process? Do you have the kind of relationship with your customers that allows them to be real and transparent with you?
* How does your purchasing and inventory control system function to minimize inventory without impacting your ability to respond to normal fluctuations in customer demand? What kind of relationships have you built with your suppliers? Do you have Kanban systems in place?
* How is your accounts payable system configured? What is your average number of days outstanding? Do you know who your problem customers are, and do you have the relationship with them to be able to work things out amicably?
* How effective is your hiring process? Are you hiring the right skill sets? More importantly, are you hiring the right kinds of personalities?

Here are some basic suggestions for creating systems, procedures, and processes that will give you a competitive edge and allow you to both delight your customers and devastate your competition.

* First and foremost, you must develop a culture where you and your employees think of virtually everything in your business in terms of its impact on your customers.

- Systems, procedures, and processes must be documented. No exceptions!
- Keep your systems and processes as simple and clear as possible.
- Commit to regularly reviewing and continually improving and stream-lining your systems.
- Always evaluate new systems and potential changes in light of their impact on your customers and your competition
  - Will it improve quality?
  - Will it reduce costs?
  - Will it speed delivery?
  - Will it delight the customer?
  - Will it bring in more business?
  - Will it give you a competitive advantage in the marketplace and allow you to grab a larger percentage of one or more markets?
  - Is it the right thing to do, etchically, morally, and financially?

APPENDIX FOUR
Paradigms

As illustrated in chapter Fourteen, businesses that miss fundamental paradigm shifts related to them can suffer severe consequences. Sometimes it's a loss of revenue, customers, or market share – but sometimes it's devastating and is enough to drown the organization and put it out of business.

Paradigms can impact a number of areas of your business:

- An advancement in product development that obsoletes your current design
- A key competitor shifting from a "make to order" to a "make to stock" operation in a market that has always been a custom arena
- Development of a new manufacturing technology that dramatically changes the cost structure of a product
- New or enhanced product features (or marketing) that gives your competition a leading edge
- Changes in customer needs or wants – either through their own demands or because someone is deliberately leading them in a new direction
- Impact of local, national, and global economic changes on things like the value of currency and your ability to stay liquid and fund ongoing operations
- Changes in the regulatory environment
- Changes in import/export laws and costs

The list could go on for pages and I'm sure that you have a least six more items that you can add right now.

The question is, "What do we do?"

Here are some ideas:

- Always be thinking about what's next
- Develop creative teams in all aspects of your business and allow them time each week to look for new and better ways to do things

- Become a lifelong learner and constantly study things related to your business, products, and the markets you serve
- Always think of potential paradigm shifts in terms of:
  - How they will impact the products and services you offer
  - How they will impact the way you do business
  - How they will impact the customers you serve

Remember the following statements and burn them indelibly into your brain:

The only constant, in life and in business, is change. You can be ahead of the curve and prosper, or you can be behind the curve and suffer. The choice is yours.

APPENDIX FIVE
Technology

Technology comes in all shapes and sizes, so I could write an entire book about the proper selection and application of technology as it relates to your business and your customers.

Consider the following examples:

- Production technology and how it impacts cycle time and overall cost. (This does not just apply to manufacturing companies. If you are a printing house, think about the speed of your copy machines.)
- Workflow technology for creating the shortest path from start to finish in each process area of your business.
- The cost, efficiency, effectiveness, and reliability of the technology in your computer, internet, and audio/video conferencing systems.
- POS (Point Of Sale) terminals and software and their impact on the customer experience.
- Purchasing and inventory technology
- Financial technology
- Sales, marketing, and customer service software
- Mobile technology and staying connected
- Website and social media technology

Again, I'm sure you can add to this list, but you get my point about how technology impacts everything we do and has a profound effect on our ability to delight our customers.

When it comes to the appropriate procurement and use of technology, consider asking yourself the following questions:

- Is your current technology excellently serving your customers?
- Is your current technology effectively and efficiently serving your employees?
- Do you see or sense any level of "technology frustration" from your customers and/or your employees?

- Have you received any internal or external complaints about your technology?
- Are you using the latest equipment and do you have a replacement plan for upgrading both your hardware and software?
- Is all of your software at the latest revision level?
- Is your website customer friendly? Has it been designed for ease of use and minimum clicks so that your customers can easily find what they want?
- Do your website and social media offer both existing and new customers an easy way to communicate with you, and are you "extremely responsive" to the communications you receive?
- Is the development and implementation of technology part of your overall business plan and strategy?

APPENDIX SIX
People

In this final appendix, I want to focus on two primary concepts:

1. Caring for and developing your current employees
2. Hiring the right future employees

Caring for and developing your employees

Every customer-centric business ultimately springs from company leadership teams that have learned to be employee-centric. If we don't care about our employees and show that caring through relationship development, honest and open communication, and the provision of opportunities to learn, grow, and advance – then we have no right to demand that our employees do everything in their power to care for our customers.

This last statement may sound harsh, but it's true. You can demand anything you want from your employees, but that doesn't mean that you're going to get it – especially when your back is turned or you are out of the office. When people feel that they **have** to do something, instead of **wanting** to do it, even if the execution is proper, the attitude of real "customer service from the heart" is usually missing. And you're a fool if you think your customers don't see it and feel it.

Here are some key ideas for building a team that will become customer-centric:

- Employees want to feel valued
- Employees want to be respected for who they are and the work they do
- Employees want to be appreciated for the efforts they put forth in the performance of their duties
- Employees want to be trusted by the leaders and owners of the businesses for which they work
- Employees want to be able to trust their leaders and business owners
- Trust and respect are earned, not demanded

- Employees need a feeling of belonging
- Employees need to understand where they fit in (i.e. how what they do matters to both the business and the customer)
- Employees need the opportunity to grow, progress, and continue to learn new and diverse skill sets
- Employees want to contribute to the well being of the enterprise
- Employees enjoy delighting customers
- Employees have great ideas for new products and new ways to do things. They need to be heard and given credit for the good ideas they put forward.
- When their ideas are not accepted, employees need to know why, and they need to be respected and encouraged to keep the ideas coming

Take these ideas into consideration when you are planning your "customer-centric initiative". They can help you lay the foundation for an amazing future.

Hiring the right future employees

Customer-centric businesses are employee-centric. I've already said that enough times that you're probably sick of hearing it. But here's a new twist:

Employee-centric businesses attract a certain kind of individual

That's right. Truly employee-centric organizations have typically created a very unique dynamic, or culture, of engagement and participation. They also are much more likely to operate at entirely different levels of both energy and creativity compared to their run of the mill competitors. As a result, hiring new employees becomes a unique challenge for the leaders of these companies.

So how do you best deal with bringing new people into your growing, employee-centric, customer-centric business?

- Hire the personality along with the resume. This simply means that the personality of those you hire is often as important, if not more so, than their credentials and experience.

- From a personality perspective, have a clear understanding of the kind of person who will best fit the organizational culture you and your employees have created.
- Ask the tough questions and use situational analysis to ferret out the person you are seeking. A neat example of this comes from a friend of mine who works in a heavily customer-focused business. As part of the interviewing process, her company often stages situations for someone coming in for an interview. One time, they had a woman in the parking lot struggling to put something into her car when the interviewee arrived. One person from the company went to the parking lot to meet and escort the interviewee into the building. The test was to determine if the person had such a heart for helping others that he would ask the company representative to wait while he helped the woman put the object into her car.
- Involve your employees in the process, especially those with whom the new individual will be directly working. You do this (a) because it's the right thing to do and (b) because employee-centric businesses are places of employee involvement.
- Don't be cheap in your hiring process. If you find a person who is the right fit, pay a little extra to get them on board. The return on your investment will be far beyond the little bit of money it costs you.

Use all of these ideas to the health, happiness, and success of your enterprise!

www.ingramcontent.com/pod-product-compliance
Lightning Source LLC
Chambersburg PA
CBHW022029090426
42739CB00006BA/353